I'd Rather Be Playing Golf Cookbook

I'd Rather Be Playing Golf Cookbook

Gilli Davies

Illustrations by Rick Havely

ISBN 978-09562198-0-0

Cover design by Clare Brayshaw

Cover illustration by Rick Havely

Prepared by:

York Publishing Services Ltd,
64 Hallfield Road,
Layerthorpe,
York
YO31 7ZQ
Telephone 01904 431213

www.yps-publishing.co.uk

About the author

Gilli Davies

Gilli has worked with food, and as a restaurateur, broadcaster and food writer for over 20 years. She has played golf for 5 years. Guess which comes first in her life now!

Gilli's cookery books range from a Taste of Cyprus, Welsh Calendar Cookbook, Cook Organic and most recently Celtic Cuisine. Her TV series, Tastes of Wales was shown on BBC Wales, BBC 2, BBC Worldwide and Cable TV. She lives in north Yorkshire running cookery classes from her home, when not on the golf course.

www.gillidavies.co.uk

About the illustrator

Rik Havely

Rick left London for Crayke in North Yorkshire in the early nineties. He now works with Rural Arts North Yorkshire for whom he performs a myriad of arty techniques in workshops and projects for all sectors of the community, the length and breadth of the county.

Index

Index – continued

Why it was necessary to write this book

Golf may be an all consuming game, but golfers get very hungry, and there is a limit to just how many bacon baps a golfer can eat ......

Many golfers can swing, hook and slice well in the kitchen. However the draw of another round of golf is too great, and the desire to cook fades away.

Quick, simple and very delicious food is what every golfer wants at the end of a round. And few want their games ruined by the troublesome thought of how to achieve this perfect meal while out on the course.

This book can guarantee a stress free game of golf, because supper is sorted, even if the golf isn't.

It's all down to the planning and timing.

Plan what goes into the golf bag, and make a shopping list at the same time. Once the ingredients are in the kitchen at home, you can linger on the 19th.

Score a hole in one. Play golf and eat well afterwards.

Similar to yardage on the golf course, measurements are in imperial with metric in brackets.

All recipes are for 4.

How this cook book works

These 18 menus are based on when you play your game of golf during the day.

Menu 1 will suit the early golfer and menu 18 is for the late player.

A round of 18 holes of golf takes generally between 4 and 5 hours.

PLAYING EARLY? There's no time to prepare a meal before you head for the first tee. Afterwards though, there should be time to put something special together. Just make sure the shopping is done and the ingredients are in the fridge.

PLAYING THROUGH MIDDAY? Start the preparation before you go out, and finish the cooking when you get in.

PLAYING LATE? You'll need a meal absolutely ready to dive into at the end of the day.

Some menus have a starter and main course and others have a main course and pudding.

Whatever the menu though, delaying tactics are vital, and so there is a section on nibbles etc at the beginning of the book. And a small chapter on how to numb the effects of a bad game afterwards!

Dedication

I would like to dedicate this book to the girls at
Easingwold Golf Club.

Niblicks and Tee Time Treats

Roast Salted Nuts

Put a handful of mixed nuts into a frying pan with a tablespoon of oil. Heat the nuts until they begin to sizzle then add a good pinch of salt, cajun spices and dried mixed herbs. Toss well, pour into a serving bowl and leave to cool.

Cheese Straws

In a processor, mix 4oz (100g) plain flour with 2oz (50g) butter, 2oz (50g) mature cheddar cheese, 1oz (25g) parmesan, a pinch of cayenne pepper, 1 egg yolk and 1 tablespoon of water.

Roll the dough out and cut into straw shapes.

Bake at 200°C for 8–10 minutes.

Aubergine Dip

1 large aubergine
1 clove garlic, crushed with salt
1 tablespoon tahini paste
1 small lemon, squeezed juice
a pinch of ground cumin
salt and pepper
some finely chopped parsley
a few black olives to garnish

Slice the aubergine lengthways in half and cook under the grill or on a barbecue until the skin blackens and blisters.

Spoon the aubergine flesh out of the charred skin and puree with the garlic, tahini paste, lemon juice and cumin. Season to taste.

Pile the mixture into a bowl and garnish with chopped parsley and olives.

Serve with some warm pitta bread.

Caddie Cakes

8oz (225g) self raising flour
4oz (100g) butter
3oz (75g) caster sugar
3oz (75g) currants
½ teaspoon mixed spice
1 teaspoon honey
1 egg, beaten

Rub the butter into the flour.

Add the sugar, currants, mixed spice and honey. Mix to a firm dough with the beaten egg.

Roll out or pat the mixture until it is ¼" thick.

Cut into discs and griddle over medium heat until golden on both sides. Dust with caster sugar.

Muesli Squares

1 tablespoon honey
2 tablespoons vegetable oil
2oz (50g) butter
2oz (50g) dark, soft brown sugar
3oz (75g) plain wholemeal flour
3oz (75g) rolled oats
1oz (25g) wheatgerm
2oz (50) dried apricots, finely chopped
2oz (50g) sultanas
2oz (50g) sunflower seeds

Heat the oven to 170°C. Grease a small swiss roll tin 7" x 11".

Heat the honey, oil, butter and sugar gently in a pan until melted then stir in the remaining ingredients.

Press into the swiss roll tin and bake for 20 minutes until golden.

Cut into squares while still warm.

Date Shortbread

8oz (225g) plain flour
1 teaspoon baking powder
6oz (175g) butter
4oz (100g) soft brown sugar
6oz (175g) chopped dates

Rub the butter into the flour with the baking powder.

Add the sugar and chopped dates and mix well

Press the mixture into a shallow baking tray so that it is about ½" thick.

Bake at 180°C for 30–40 minutes.

Cut into fingers while still warm and dust with caster sugar.

1st Hole......

The early birdie – and no time to think about supper.
Just make sure the ingredients are ready for later.
The salad can be thrown together in minutes and the salmon and
couscous should take no longer than 20 minutes. Salmon tails are
inexpensive and boneless.

Tomato, Mozzarella and Basil Scramble

6-8 large ripe plum tomatoes
8oz (225g) buffalo mozzarella
a good bunch of basil leaves

Vinaigrette

3 tablespoons virgin olive oil
1 tablespoon white wine or cider vinegar
1 teaspoon wholegrain mustard
1 teaspoon honey
salt and pepper

Slice the tomatoes and arrange on 4 plates. Slice the mozzarella and arrange the slices between the tomatoes.

Tear the basil leaves into small pieces and scatter over.

Mix all the ingredients for the dressing and drizzle on top.

Serve with salad with chunks of fresh bread, or warm pitta.

Cajun Salmon Wedges with Couscous

1½ lb (675g) salmon tails, skin on
1 tablespoon light oil
2 teaspoons Cajun spices
1 lemon for garnish
7oz (200g) couscous

Rub the Cajun spices into the flesh side of the salmon tails.

Heat a griddle pan to a medium heat and put in the salmon tails, skin side underneath. Depending on their thickness, cook for 5-10 minutes, or until you can see that the flesh is cooked about half way through.

Turn the salmon over, so that the spices are now sizzling in the pan and continue to cook until the salmon flesh is cooked right through.

Remove from the pan, strip off the skin and serve the salmon with any juices from the pan poured over.

Garnish with wedges of lemon and serve with couscous.

Couscous is pre-cooked durum wheat semolina and needs only to be soaked in boiling water. So put the couscous in a heatproof dish and pour over 9 fl oz (250ml) of boiling water, adding a knob of butter and a dash of salt to taste.

Cover and leave for 5-10 minutes until the water has been fully absorbed.

Separate the grains with a fork before serving.

Chicken on the Green

2 tablespoons rapeseed or light oil
4 chicken breasts, skinned and boned
8 spring onions, chopped, or 2 small leeks, sliced and washed
2 cloves garlic, crushed
1 teaspoon finely grated fresh root ginger
1 lb (450g) spinach, well washed
1 tablespoon tamari or light soy sauce
salt and freshly ground black pepper
toasted sesame seeds, for garnish

Heat the oil in a heavy-based casserole and fry the chicken breasts for 2-3 minutes on each side until they begin to colour. Remove and add the spring onions, garlic and ginger and fry for 2 minutes, then stir in the spinach, tossing in the oil. As it begins to wilt, stir in the tamari and seasoning, then return the chicken to the pan. Cover with a lid and simmer gently for 15-20 minutes until cooked.

Bulgar Pilaff with Raisins

1 tablespoon olive oil
1 onion, chopped
6oz (175g) bulgar or cracked wheat
2oz (50g) raisins
16fl oz (450ml) boiling chicken stock
1 tablespoon chopped fresh parsley
salt and freshly ground pepper

Heat the oil and cook the onion gently till soft. Add the bulgur and stir for 1 minute to coat in the oil. Add the raisins and stock, cover and simmer over low heat for 15 minutes or until all the liquid has been absorbed. Stir in the parsley and season to taste.

Great recipe, this. An all time family favourite. Mix and cook it in a microwave bowl and there's little washing up either. The measurements are rather unusual, but they work.
It cooks ok in the oven too.

Hot Chocolate Pudding

4oz (100g) butter
2 eggs
7 teaspoons cocoa powder
1 cup (standard teacup size) caster sugar
½ cup plain flour
½ teaspoon vanilla essence

Melt the butter. Beat in the eggs, cocoa powder, sugar, flour and vanilla essence. The mixture should be quite runny.

Microwave for about 3 minutes on high in the microwave, or about 20 minutes in a tray in a medium oven.

It should still be a little runny in the middle.

Wonderful if served warm with vanilla ice cream.

Salmon in the Round

8oz (225g) good quality sliced smoked salmon
1 lb (450g) fresh salmon
½ glass dry white wine
4oz (100g) cream cheese
1 tablespoon creamed horseradish
a good squeeze of lemon juice
chopped parsley and chives for garnish

First make the salmon filling:
Steam/microwave the fresh salmon in the white wine and leave to cool. Process it with the cream cheese, horseradish and lemon to make a smooth pate. Chill.

Divide the slices of smoked salmon into 8 wide strips and roll each gently around a good dessertspoonful of the pâté.

Serve two rolls per plate and garnish with extra strips of smoked salmon, chopped parsley, olive oil and whole chives.

Serve with hot toast.

Toad in the Hole

8oz (225g) streaky bacon, rinded and diced
1 lb (450g) best quality pork sausages
2-3 leeks
½ pint (300ml) whole milk
4oz (100g) plain flour
2 eggs
1 tablespoon melted butter
salt and pepper

Heat the oven to 200°C.

Blend the ingredients for the batter using the milk, flour, eggs, butter and lots of seasoning.

In a large flattish casserole, dryfry the sausages until the fat runs and they brown. Remove from the pan and add the bacon. Cook until it begins to crisp and brown then add the leeks and cook for 3-4 minutes to soften. Return the sausages to the pan.

(if you don't have a large casserole, fry the sausages, bacon and leeks in a frying pan and transfer to a deep baking tray.).

Pour the batter around the sausages and bake for 30-40 minutes until risen, crisp and brown.

Make up some good onion gravy to pour over the toad in the hole.

Divots of Pork with Cider and Apples

1½ lbs (675g) pork fillet, sliced into 1" thick chunks
1 tablespoon olive oil
1oz (25g) butter
2 large onions, sliced
½ pint (300ml) cider
¼ pint (150ml) light stock, chicken or vegetable
2 red eating apples, sliced and cored, but not peeled
1 tablespoon chopped parsley
salt and pepper

Heat the oil and butter in a large frying pan or casserole and fry the onions until they soften. Add the pork and fry to seal on all sides.

Add the cider and the stock and bring to the boil then reduce the heat and cook very gently for 15-20 minutes.

Add the apples and cook for another 5 minutes.

Put the pork, onion and apples on to a serving dish and keep hot.

Add the parsley to the pan and boil the sauce to reduce and thicken.

Season to taste and the pour the sauce over the meat.

Potatoes could be boiled and mashed in the time it takes for the pork to cook. Alternatively, boiled noodles tossed in butter and black pepper make a great accompaniment.

Fruit Out of Bounds

1 lb (450g) stewed fruit, rhubarb, plums, apricots,
etc. sweetened but still sharp
½ pint (300ml) double cream
3 tablespoons sweet sherry, masala or sweet wine
½ pint fromage frais or greek yoghurt
1 packet ratafia biscuits

Arrange the stewed fruit in the bottom of a serving bowl.

Whisk the cream until thick but not stiff, and fold in the marsala
and yoghurt. Spread over the fruit.

Decorate with the biscuits all over the top, and chill till needed.

Caddie's Tasty Bites

A loaf of French bread
virgin olive oil
Base
6 ripe tomatoes
1 clove garlic, crushed
2 tablespoons chopped fresh herbs
Seasoning
Topping
feta cheese, black olives, anchovies

Slice the French bread thinly and rub each slice with olive oil. Arrange on a baking sheet and bake in a hot oven till crisp.

For the base
Quarter the tomatoes, scoop out the seeds and chop the flesh as finely as possible. Mix in a bowl with the crushed garlic, chopped herbs and seasoning.

For the topping
Crumble the feta cheese, stone and slice the black olives and divide the anchovy fillets lengthways.

To serve – Spoon a little of the base mixture on to each slice of toasted bread and top with feta, olives and a strip of anchovy.

Chicken to the Rescue

4 good sized chicken breasts or 8 thighs
2 cloves garlic, crushed
2 lemons, grated rind and squeezed juice
1-2 tablespoons runny honey
salt and pepper

Heat the oven to 200°C.

Arrange the chicken in a baking dish.

Mix the garlic, lemon rind and juice, honey and seasoning and pour over the chicken.

Bake for about an hour until the chicken is golden brown and cooked right through.

Potatoes with Pancetta

2 lbs (1.8kg) potatoes, peeled and sliced thinly lengthways
4oz (100g) pancetta affumicata, thinly sliced
4 tablespoons olive oil
2 cloves garlic, peeled and finely sliced
10 sage leaves
9 fl oz (250ml) double cream
salt and pepper
1oz (25g) parmesan cheese

Fry the pancetta in a little oil then add the garlic and sage and cook for a minute. Take off the heat and stir in the cream and seasoning.

In a large open ovenproof dish, layer up the potatoes with the pancetta and cream mixture. Cover with foil and bake on the shelf under the chicken for 30 minutes then uncover and continue to cook for a further 20 minutes or until the potatoes are soft. Scatter over the parmesan and return to the oven for another 5 minutes.

Eggs in the Rough

9oz (250g) new potatoes
4oz (100g) asparagus, cut into 1" lengths
4oz (100g) frozen peas
5 eggs
6oz (175g) gruyere cheese, grated
salt and freshly ground black pepper
2 tablespoons chopped fresh mint
2 tablespoons olive oil
1 onion, finely chopped
2 garlic cloves, crushed
good pinch crushed dried chillies

Boil the potatoes for 10-12 minutes, until just tender, adding the asparagus for the last few minutes. Drain and run under the cold tap to cool quickly.

Slice the potatoes.

Beat the eggs in a large bowl, season well and stir in the grated cheese, potatoes, asparagus, peas and mint.

Heat the oil in a large non-stick frying pan and add the onion and garlic. Cook for 4-5 minutes, until they soften, then stir in the chillies. Pour in the egg mixture and spread out evenly. Cook over a medium heat for 5-7 minutes, until almost set.

Finish off by putting the frying pan under a hot grill for a couple of minutes, until the top turns golden brown.

To Serve – cut into wedges and serve with salad and chutney.

Hot Berries in the Woods

1 lb (450g) frozen fruits of the forest berries
a wee drop of something alcoholic – rum, whisky or a liqueur
sugar to taste
vanilla ice cream

Thaw the berries either in the microwave or in a small pan on the stove. They should produce lots of juice.

Add sugar to taste and a wee drop of what you fancy.

Pour over vanilla ice cream and serve immediately.

7th Hole......

*Middle of the day game?
So get some preparation done before you go out,
and finish off when you get in.*

Spicy Cod Hot off the Tee

1lb (450g) cod fillet, cut into 1" cubes
12-15 scrubbed mussels (optional)
1 large onion, sliced
2 cloves garlic, crushed
½ pint (300ml) fish or vegetable stock
3 tablespoons balsamic vinegar
½ red chilli, either fresh or dried
½ tablespoon fresh rosemary, finely chopped
3 tablespoons fresh parsley, finely chopped
2 tins x 14oz (425g) chopped tomatoes
salt and freshly ground pepper
To Serve
Slices of toasted French bread, rubbed with halved cloves of
garlic plus a good dusting of fresh chopped parsley.

Combine the onion, garlic, stock, vinegar and chillies in a pan.
Cover and boil for 5-7 minutes then uncover and simmer until
the onions are tender and the liquid almost gone.

Add the herbs and cook for a minute then add the tomatoes and seasoning and simmer for 15 minutes. Leave to cool.

When you get in, reheat this tomato sauce until it boils. Add the white fish, cover with a lid and cook for 5 minutes. Add the mussels and cook for a further 2 minutes, until the shells are open.

To Serve – Place a slice of toast in 4 shallow soup bowls, ladle the fish and sauce over the toast and sprinkle with parsley.

Get this one made up in advance …

Vanilla Slice

1 large pot (500g) natural Greek yogurt
1 large pot (600ml) double cream
3 tablespoons caster sugar
5 leaves gelatine
1 teaspoon pure vanilla essence

Line a 2 lb (1kg) loaf tin with cling film.

Soak the gelatine in cold water for five minutes.

Heat ½ the cream with the sugar. Squeeze the gelatine leaves to remove the water and stir into the hot cream until dissolved.

Mix the remaining cream with the yogurt, pour in the warm cream and vanilla essence.

Whisk the mixture together to remove any lumps and pour into the prepared loaf tin.

Cover and chill for at least 8 hours.

Turn the vanilla slice out and slice. Serve with summer fruit – raspberries, strawberries or a compote of any fruits in season.

A great way to unwind after a good game of golf. Everything can be prepared in advance – that only leaves the grill to be lit.

Barbecue in the Bag

Marinade for Lamb Chops or Lamb Kebabs

2 tablespoons soy sauce
1 tablespoon honey
1 clove garlic, crushed
juice of a lemon
1 onion, chopped

Mix together and pour over the lamb.

Pork and Coriander Patties

1 lb (450g) lean pork, minced
1 onion, finely grated
2 tablespoons chopped flat leaf parsley
salt and freshly ground black pepper
2 teaspoons coriander seeds, crushed

Mix all the ingredients together then press into chubby sausage shapes. Chill well.

Barbecue, serve with wedges of lemon.

Bacon and Potato Spikes

12 small new potatoes, par boiled
6 rashers streaky bacon
1 red pepper, cut into 6 chunks
1 yellow pepper cut into 6 chunks
12 button mushrooms
2 medium courgettes, cut into 12 large slices
6 pickling onions

Cut the bacon rashers in half and stretch with the back of a knife, then wrap around each of the potatoes.

Thread all the ingredients alternatively on to 6 skewers.

BBQ Sauce

4 tablespoons tomato ketchup
2 tablespoons Worcester sauce
juice of ½ a lemon
1 teaspoon English mustard
1 dessertspoon oil
1 dessertspoon demerara sugar

Boil the following ingredients together until reduced by ⅓.

Colonel Bogey's Baked Bananas

Put some bananas in their skins on top of a cool barbecue, turn after 10 minutes and leave them to blacken on all sides.

Serve, split open with some brandy, soft brown sugar and cream poured over.

Antipasta Takeaway

Just head for the nearest delicatessen counter and collect a delicious range of cold meats, marinated vegetables and some cheese.

Or you could try this raw beef dish

It's tender and delicious – don't be put off – try it!

Beef Carpaccio

8-10oz (225g-300g) piece of beef fillet, trimmed
salt and freshly ground black pepper
4-6 tablespoons pesto mixed with 1 tablespoon olive oil
1 shallot or small onion
4 tablespoons drained capers
4oz (100g) block of parmesan cheese

Before you go out, wrap the beef in some cling film and freeze.

As soon as you get in, take the beef out of the freezer.

Using a very sharp knife, cut the beef into wafer thin slivers. Arrange on 4 large plates, overlapping the slices slightly.

Season with salt and pepper and drizzle with pesto.

Finely chop the shallot and sprinkle over the beef with the capers.

Shave thin slivers off the parmesan cheese with a vegetable peeler and scatter them carefully over the beef.

Serve with warm bread, toast or foccaccia.

Peppers Pizza Matchplay

Base
8oz (225g) self raising flour
pinch salt
1 egg
salt and pepper
½ cup olive oil
½ cup water
Topping
3 medium tomatoes, sliced
1 large onion, peeled and sliced
2-3 large peppers, seeded and sliced
½ cup olive oil
salt and pepper
Mediterranean herbs

Prepare the topping by mixing all the prepared vegetables in a bowl with the olive oil, herbs and seasoning. Leave for a couple of hours if possible.

When you get in, heat the oven to 200°C.

For the base, put the flour into a bowl and mix in the other ingredients with enough water to make a soft dough.

Press the dough into a deep oiled baking tin and scatter over the vegetables and herbs, pouring all the oil over too.

Bake for 45 minutes to an hour until the vegetables begin to char and the dough is crisp at the edges.

10th Hole......

This is a real success. How could it be so easy!

Salmon Bread and Putter Pudding

6 slices white bread, crusts off, spread with garlic butter
1 small glass dry white wine
1lb (450g) fresh fillet of salmon, sliced thinly
6 eggs
salt and pepper
2 tablespoons each chopped dill and chives
5 fl oz (140ml) milk + 5 fl oz (140ml) single cream

Arrange half the bread in the bottom of a baking dish. Pour over the wine.

Arrange the slices of salmon across the dish with the rest of the bread on top.

Whisk the eggs, seasoning, herbs, milk and cream together and pour over the pudding.

This dish can now be left in the fridge until you get in. The watercress vinaigrette can be made in advance too.

Bake at 190°C for 20-25 minutes.

Watercress Vinaigrette

Liquidise a bunch of watercress with some french dressing.

Serve with a mixed green salad.

Bunkered Fruit

Use any of the following fruit

figs
bananas
oranges
apples
pears
grapes
strawberries
raspberries
peaches
apricots
plums

Arrange the fruit, whole or sliced, so that all the pieces are roughly the same size, in a flat baking dish. Leave in the fridge until later.

Scatter over some demerara or soft brown sugar and pop into the oven as soon as the bread and butter pudding comes out.

Turn the oven to 220°C and cook for about 20 minutes until the sugar begins to caramelise.

Serve warm with cream or ice cream.

Although there isn't much to be done beforehand, apart from making sure you have all the ingredients ready, this recipe takes no time to throw together.

Green Fees't with Chicken and Bacon

4 chicken breasts
1 tablespoon light oil
A good selection of mixed salad leaves, including rocket, washed and dried
4oz (100g) dry cured bacon, cut into strips
1 shallot or small onion, finely diced
2oz (50g) pinenuts
1 tablespoon wine or cider vinegar
2 tablespoons best quality olive oil
seasoning
1oz (25g) freshly grated parmesan

Open out the chicken breasts so that they are as flat as possible, then pan fry gently in a little oil until golden brown on all sides and cooked right through.

Arrange the salad leaves on 4 large plates.

Dry fry the bacon until the fat runs then add the shallot and cook till soft.

Toss in the pinenuts.

Season well, stir in the vinegar and extra olive oil and pour at once over the salad. Scatter over the parmesan.

Serve with warm rolls or foccaccia to soak up the juices.

Meringue with Lots of Loft

1 lemon, grated rind
2 tablespoon caster sugar
1oz (25g) butter
3/4 pint (450ml) milk
6oz (175g) fresh white breadcrumbs
3 egg yolks
4oz (100g) raspberries or strawberries or 2 tabs raspberry jam
For the meringue topping
3 egg whites
3 tablespoons caster sugar

Add the lemon rind, sugar and butter to the milk and bring to the boil.

Pour this mixture over the breadcrumbs and leave to stand for 10 minutes.

Stir the egg yolks into the cooled bread mixture and spoon into a 4 ramekin dishes.

Arrange the sliced fruit or jam over the surface and chill.

Whisk the egg whites till very stiff. Fold in the sugar and swirl the meringue on top of the puddings.

Bake at 180°C until the meringue is golden and crisp – 10-15 minutes.

Serve warm with cream, ice cream or custard.

Game with Rough Potatoes

4 x 6oz (175g) venison loin steaks
1 teaspoon coriander seeds, crushed
1 glass red wine
2 tablespoons sunflower oil
juice of ½ an orange
1 teaspoon redcurrant jelly
salt and freshly ground black pepper
For the Rosti
2 large potatoes
1 medium leek
salt and freshly ground pepper

Add the coriander seeds to the wine and pour over the venison. Leave to marinade while you are chasing the little white ball.

For the rosti
Peel and grate the potato and leek and season well. Cook this mixture as soon as you can to stop it discolouring.

Heat a tablespoon of oil in a large pan and fry four mounds of the rosti mixture gently, turning once to brown both sides. Take out of the pan and keep warm.

Heat the remaining oil and fry the venison steaks briskly to seal on both sides then lower the heat and cook for 4 minutes until cooked but pink in the middle.

Dish a rosti onto each serving plate, slice the venison steaks and arrange on top.

Add the marinade to the pan juices and stir well then add the orange juice and redcurrant jelly and boil to reduce by half.

Taste for seasoning and pour around the steaks.

Easy Swing Trifle

3 slices Panetone cake with cut peel
2 tablespoons Marsala/sweet dessert wine
4oz (100g) ready to eat dried apricots, chopped
1 glass orange juice
1 pint (600ml) thick custard
½ pint (300ml) double cream
Amaretti biscuits

Soak the apricots in a glass of orange juice for an hour. Arrange the Panetone slices over the bottom of an attractive bowl. Pour over the Marsala to soak in. Scatter the apricots over the sponge. Pour over the custard to cover completely. Chill well before covering with the gently whisked double cream.

Decorate the top with crumbled Amaretti biscuits.

13th Hole......

Make up the Blini ahead, and top with cream and smoked salmon just before you want them.

Dill Blini with Smoked Salmon Topping

2oz (50g) self raising flour
1 egg
1 tablespoon chopped dill
1 tablespoon melted butter
salt and pepper
milk

Put the flour in a bowl and with a fork or whisk add the eggs, dill, butter, seasoning and enough milk to a make a thickish batter.

Drop spoonfuls into a warm buttered frying pan and griddle over medium heat until coloured on both sides.

Serve with crème fraiche or sour cream mixed with horseradish cream.

Top with strips of smoked salmon.

Such a useful dish, this. Prepare ahead and pop it into the oven as soon as you get in.

Birdie Bake

A good bowlful of cooked and chopped chicken
3 heads of broccoli (roughly equivalent in volume to the chicken)
2 tins of Campbell's mushroom condensed soup
½ a small jar of mayonnaise
½ a teaspoon of curry powder
juice of a lemon
a dash of milk
4oz (100g) strong Cheddar cheese, grated
salt & pepper

Parboil the broccoli, drain, chill and place in an oven-proof dish. Add the cooked chicken.

Mix together the soup, mayonnaise, curry powder, lemon juice and milk until you get a fairly loose sauce. Season with salt and plenty of black pepper.

Pour the sauce over the chicken and broccoli and sprinkle the top with the grated Cheddar. Chill.

Heat the oven to 200°C and bake for 30-40 minutes until browned on top.

Serve with pasta, rice or jacket potatoes.

Both these dishes benefit from being made early in the day and left to stand for the flavours to improve.

Putted Trout

8 trout fillets, boned
½ glass of dry white wine
a good pinch of salt
a pinch of cayenne
a good pinch of powdered mace
a few drops of anchovy essence
3-4 tablespoons of thick cream

Poach the trout fillets in the wine (preferably in the microwave on medium power for 7 minutes), then leave to cool.

Pound or process all the ingredients to make a smooth, moist and tasty mixture.

Press into small jars or ramekins and pour clarified butter over the top. (*Melt some butter until it separates and use the clear butter on top*)

Leave for about 5 hours before serving with hot toast.

Big Bean Masters

8oz (225g) streaky smoked bacon
4 good sized leeks, sliced and washed
3 cloves garlic, crushed
2 tins mixed beans
2 tins chopped tomatoes
chilli pepper, to taste
1 Toulouse or fat Chorizo sausage, sliced
1-2 smoked ducks breasts, sliced
4 slices bread, crumbled
1oz (25g) butter

In a large heavy based casserole fry the bacon until the fat runs. Add the leeks and cook till soft, then add 2 cloves of garlic. Now toss in the beans, tomatoes, chilli, sausage and duck. Cover and cook gently for an hour at 180°C. Season to taste after cooking, but take care with the salt.

Melt the butter in a frying pan and fry the remaining garlic until golden, add the breadcrumbs and cook till crisp. Scatter the crumbs over the casserole and leave to cool.

On returning from the golf course, heat on top of the stove while the oven is heating then bake for ½ hour at 200°C until the top is golden.

Lamb Shanks Four

4 lamb shanks
1 large onion, sliced
2 carrots, peeled and sliced
2 sticks of celery, chopped
1 clove garlic, crushed
handful of fresh thyme
¼ bottle white wine
For the topping;
Mix 2 tablespoons chopped parsley
grated rind of 2 lemons
1 crushed clove of garlic

In a large frying pan or casserole, fry the lamb shanks fast to brown all over.

Remove from the pan and add the onions, carrots, celery and garlic and cook till they colour. Add the thyme, white wine and seasoning and boil up well.

Return the lamb to the pan, cover and cook very slowly for a couple of hours until the meat is tender. Leave to cool.

Skim off any fat as you reheat the casserole and sprinkle over the topping just before serving.

Brassie of Berries in Champagne Jelly

12 fl oz (350ml) champagne or sparkling dry white wine
9oz (250g) caster sugar
1 x 11g packet powdered gelatine or 2 sheets leaf gelatine
a mixture of best quality soft fruit: strawberries, raspberries,
redcurrants, blueberries, etc.

Heat the champagne with the sugar and stir until the sugar has dissolved.

Soak the gelatine in cold water to soften then add to the wine. Leave the mixture to cool, then chill until it is on the verge of setting.

Use 4-6 (depending of size) individual dariole moulds or ramekins and arrange a layer of soft fruit across the bottom. Pour in enough cold jelly to just cover the fruit and return the mould to the fridge to set.

Once this layer has set add another layer of fruit and jelly and continue like this until the mould is full.

Chill the jellies before serving.

Albatross Dream Fishcakes

Fish and potatoes mashed together can be dull and heavy, but these fishcakes have a light texture and are very tasty. They can be made from a combination of any fish, but the crabmeat really works very well. Buy it in a tin for ease.

1lb (450g) white fish, haddock, cod, coley etc
8oz (225g) crabmeat
2 eggs, beaten
5oz (150g) fresh breadcrumbs
1 stem fresh lemongrass, finely chopped
1 teaspoon French mustard, Worcestershire sauce and
Cajun spices
2 tablespoons chopped fresh parsley
light olive oil for frying

Mix all the ingredients together thoroughly.

Divide into small patties and chill for a couple of hours.

Shallow fry the fish cakes in hot until golden brown on both sides, about 5-6 minutes.

Serve hot with lemon wedges, mayonnaise and a garnish of watercress.

Pork Pitch and Chip with Courgettes

1½ lbs (700g) lean pork, cut into cubes
2 tablespoons light olive oil
2 large red onions, sliced
1 clove garlic, crushed
a good sprig of sage
½ bottle white wine
seasoning
1 lb (450g) courgettes
4oz (100g) cheddar cheese, grated
1oz (25g) parmesan cheese, grated

Heat a heavy casserole with the oil and toss in the pork cubes to brown. Remove, lower the heat and cook the onion until soft. Add the garlic, sage, seasoning, white wine and bring to the boil then return the pork to the casserole.

Simmer for about an hour until the pork is tender. Leave to cool.

For the Courgette Topping
Later arrange sliced courgettes and cheese on top of the pork and bake for 30 minutes at 200°C.

Beef Driver with Horseradish Mashie

2lbs (1kg) stewing beef, cut into 2" cubes
1 onion, sliced
4oz (100g) of unsliced smoked bacon, cut into strips
olive oil
1 bouquet garni
2oz (50g) pitted black olives or tapenade
For the marinade
1 pint red wine, 2 diced carrots, 1 sliced onion, 2 cloves,
a bay leaf, a few slices of leek, zest of ½ orange and a
tablespoon of olive oil

Mix the marinade ingredients. Add the meat and leave overnight.

Next day drain the meat, keeping the marinade. Sauté the onion in a tablespoon of olive oil until soft then lightly brown the meat and add the smoked bacon. Transfer the meat to a large casserole or slow cooker.

Bring the marinade to the boil, add half a pint of water and the bouquet garni, boil for 10 minutes then strain. Add to the meat, onions and bacon, season to taste and cook very very gently for two hours. Leave to cool.

Reheat on top of the stove for speed and stir in the black olives or 2 tablespoons of tapenade.

Serve with boiled potatoes which have been mashed with a good tablespoonful of creamed horseradish. (These could be prepared well ahead and reheated in the microwave.)

This is a stunning pudding, well worth the effort

Strawberry Roulade Major

whites of 4 large eggs
6oz (175g) castor sugar
1 teaspoon ground cinnamon
1oz (25g) flaked almonds
Filling
½ pint (300ml) double cream
8oz (225g) strawberries
3 tablespoons strawberry or other liqueur

Preheat the oven to 190°C.

Line a swiss roll tin with a double layer of greaseproof paper.

Whisk the egg whites until standing in stiff peaks. Keep a tablespoon of the sugar aside and whisk in the rest little by little until the meringue is thick and shiny. Spread the meringue into the lined tin. Sprinkle over the flaked almonds. Mix together the reserved sugar and cinnamon and sprinkle on top.

Bake for 10-12 minutes or until firm to touch. Turn out (over) on to parchment paper and leave to cool.

Whisk the cream until stiff and add the liqueur.

For the Filling
Spread the cream over the meringue and top with sliced strawberries. From one long side, roll up the meringue and transfer to a serving dish. Chill and decorate with a few slices of strawberries just before serving.

Sauce
Blend 8oz (225g) fresh strawberries with a small glass of elderflower or apple juice.

Tagine of Lamb to the Fore

2 lbs (900g) lean lamb
3 onions, sliced
2 clove of garlic, crushed
1oz (25g) butter
½ teaspoon salt
1 teaspoon ground ginger
½ teaspoon saffron
1 stick cinnamon
1 pint of water
1 tin chopped tomatoes
1 teaspoon honey
8oz (225g) pre-soaked prunes or apricots
2oz (50g) flaked almonds
7oz (200g) couscous
fresh coriander leaves

Combine the first 9 ingredients in a large casserole and cook gently for 50-60 minutes.

Remove the lamb and boil the liquid down until reduced by two thirds. Add the tomatoes and simmer until reduced by half, then add the honey, prunes or apricots, almonds and the lamb back into the sauce and heat through until boiling. Leave the tagine to cool until required.

Reheat the lamb either on top of the stove or in the oven or microwave, meanwhile put the couscous in a heatproof dish and pour over 9 fl oz (250ml) of boiling water, adding a knob of butter and a dash of salt to taste.

Cover and leave for 5-10 minutes until the water has been fully absorbed. Separate the grains with a fork before serving.

Reheat the tagine on top of the stove and scatter over coriander leaves before serving.

Mango and Lime in Cool Lies

1 large pot double cream
1 large pot plain yoghurt
2 limes, grated rind and squeezed juice
2 ripe mangoes, peeled, de-stoned and pureed
sugar to taste
(don't leave it too sharp or some flavour will be lost)

Whisk the cream until thick but not stiff, add the remaining ingredients and fold in gently.

Freeze the ice cream till firm.

Serve with crisp biscuits.

19th Hole......

Now that supper is sorted, you can afford to linger a little longer on the 19th. Why not try something a little different.

Mulligan's Mystery

1 measure port
½ pint orange quencher

Parr Excellance

Glass of best champagne
Tot of brandy
Dash of blackcurrant cordial

The Rider Cup

1 tot sweet martini
1 tot campari
top up with tonic
Slice of lemon

Whisky Gimme

2 tots whisky
top with ginger ale
Few dashes angustura bitters

Celebration 'Hole in One' ...

Breast of Duck with Plums

4 duck breasts
2 tablespoons balsamic vinegar
1 tablespoon honey
6-8 good sized plums, halved and stoned
½ teaspoon allspice berries, crushed
Salt and freshly ground black pepper

Heat a large, flameproof casserole and gently cook the duck breasts, skin side down, until the fat melts and the skin crisps and turns golden. Drain off excess fat.

Add the vinegar, honey, plums, allspice and seasoning. Cover and cook gently for 15-20 minutes.

Remove the duck breasts and cut into slices. Arrange on top of a mound of potato and celeriac puree on warmed individual plates or down the centre of a large serving dish.

Drain off the excess fat from the casserole, bring the remaining juices to the boil and reduce down to a syrupy consistency. Spoon the sauce around the duck.

Potato and Celeriac Puree

Peel an equal amount of potatoes and celeriac. Boil them together until soft. Mash with butter, milk and lots of seasoning.

Weights & Measures

Weights

1oz	25g
2oz	50g
3oz	75g
4oz	100-120g
5oz	150g
6oz	175g
7oz	200g
8oz	225g
9oz	250g
10oz	300g
11oz	325g
12oz	350g
1lb	450g
1½ lbs	675g
2 lbs	900g
3 lbs	1.35kg

Liquid Measures

1 fl oz	25ml	
2 fl oz	50ml	
3 fl oz	75-85ml	
4 fl oz	100-125ml	
5 fl oz	150ml	(¼ pint)
10 fl oz	300ml	(½ pint)
15 fl oz	425ml	(3/4 pint)
20 fl oz	575ml	1 pint
35 fl oz	1 ltr	(13/4 pint)
	1.1 ltr	2 pints

Oven Temperatures

Centigrade			
Electric	*Fan Oven*	*Gas*	
130	120	½	very cool
140	130	1	cool
150	140	2	cool
160	150	3	moderate
180	160	4	moderate
190	160	5	fairly hot
200	170	6	fairly hot
220	180	7	hot
230	190	8	very hot
240	190	9	very hot

Forthcoming titles in this series by I'd Rather Be … Cookbooks

I'd Rather Be Eating Local Food

I'd Rather Be Fishing

I'd Rather Be In The Garden

I'd Rather Be Sailing

Extra Recipes

Order more copies from www.gillidavies.co.uk